SCARLATTI

THE FIRST BOOK FOR PIANISTS

Edited by

Margery Halford

Domenico Scarlatti (1685 - 1757)
Lithograph by Alfred Lemoine

CONTENTS

K. refers to the numbers assigned to Scarlatti's works by Ralph Kirkpatrick.

L. refers to the numbers assigned by Allesandro Longo.

L.S. refers to the Supplement to the Longo edition.

The selections included in this book are taken from "SCARLATTI — An Introduction to his Keyboard Works." For students and teachers who prefer an expanded introductory section and additional selections in a 64 page book, the publisher recommends the Scarlatti introduction listed above.

This volume contains the very easiest pieces by Domenico Scarlatti. The repertoire for the young pianist always needs short, pleasing pieces which develop fine musicianship along with good technique. Scarlatti's music is ideal for these purposes. In addition, the young pianist who is not familiar with Scarlatti will find them an unexpected delight because of their always-fresh sound. Scarlatti himself was a teacher of young people, and his writing shows that he knew what would please them.

Although Scarlatti's works were composed for the harpsichord, he made so many innovations in technique and developed it with so much ingenuity, that he has been called the father of modern piano technique. The young pianist will find the modest technical challenges in these easy pieces pleasing to surmount because of their delightful sound.

There has long been a need for a collection of these pieces in an edition which presents them in their original form, without inaccuracies or the addition of unsuitable performance suggestions. In restoring them to their original purity, this volume has been thoroughly researched from the manuscript copies in

(continued on page 24)

MINUETTO

K.73b; L.217

(a) It is impossible to determine where some of the slurs in the Venice manuscript begin and end. The very clear ones have provided sufficient information to write the remaining ones in conformity with customary performance practices.

(b) See the discussion on page 24.

ⓒ The *piano* indication is one of the very few dynamic markings in the original manuscripts.

SONATA

K.34; L.S.7

Larghetto M.M. ♩ = 80~100

ARIA

K, 32; L, 423

(a) All of the trills in this *Aria* may be played with more repercussions or without terminations. See the discussion on page 24.

MINUETTO

Allegro M.M. ♩ = 120-126

K.42; L.S.36

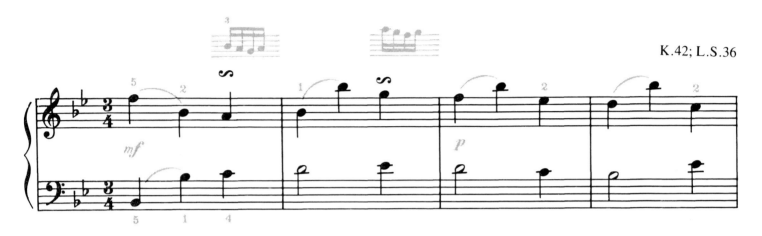

(a) The trills may have more repercussions or terminations. See the discussion on page 24.

SONATA

Allegro M. M. ♪ = 120 - 138

K.90d; L.106

(a) Other styles in which the trills may be played are discussed on page 24.

D. C.

MINUET

Allegro M.M. ♪ = 144-168

K.83b; L.S.31

(a) See page 24 for a discussion of other styles in which the trills may be played.

13

MINUET

Allegro M.M. ♪ = 120-132

K.77b; L.168

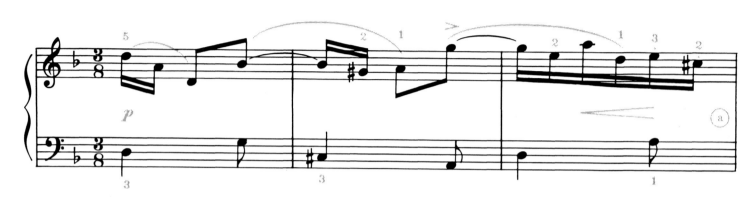

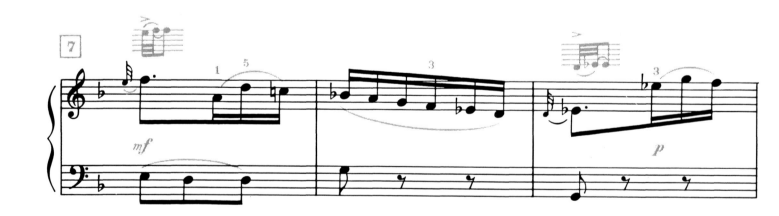

(a) Longo has inserted the following measure between measures 3 and 4. It is not in the Venice manuscript.

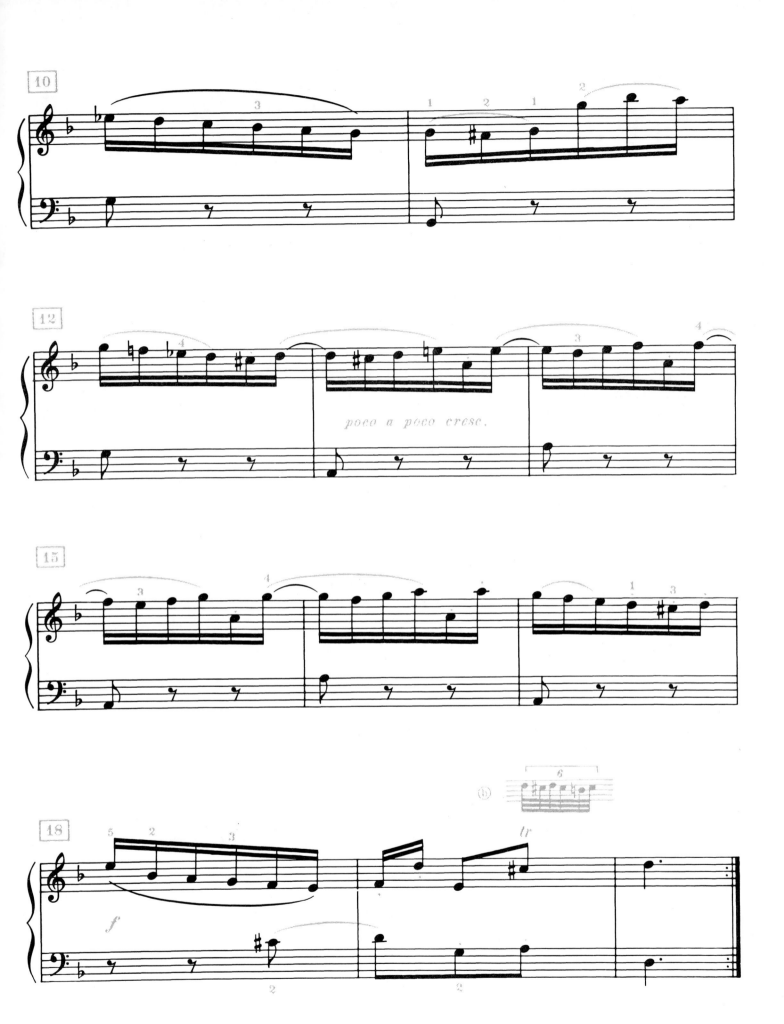

ⓑ Different styles in which this trill and the trill in measure 39 may be played are discussed on page 24.

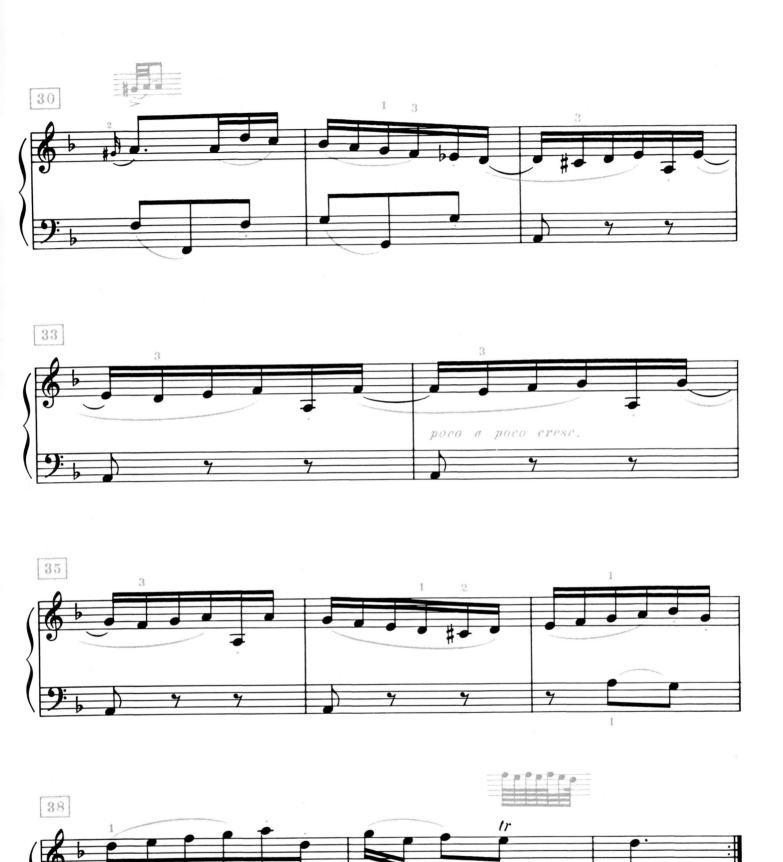

D. C.

SONATA

Allegro M.M. ♩ = 96-112

K.431; L.83

a) The rhythm of the eighths in this measure should be altered to accomodate to the prevailing triplets as shown in light print. The trill may have more repercussions. See the discussion on page 24.

PASTORAL

Allegro M.M. ♩. = 96-116

K.415; L.S.11

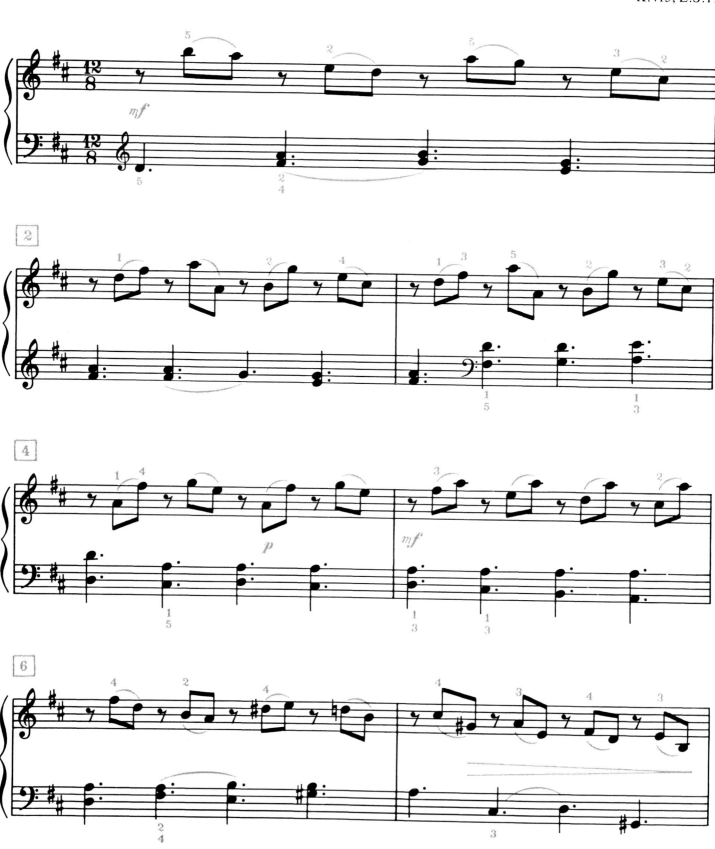

ⓐ The trills may be played with more repercussions. See the discussion on page 24.

(continued from page 1)

Venice and Parma and all the known printed editions which appeared during or shortly after Scarlatti's lifetime. Everything in dark print is copied from the manuscripts. The light print has been added by the editor as a convenience to the performer.

STYLE AND INTERPRETATION

The phrasing and staccatos in light print in this book show how music composed during Scarlatti's lifetime was performed. The style is mostly half-detached, with short groups of slurred notes. Dissonances and syncopated rhythms are accented. This baroque style of playing brings out the sparkle and Spanish flavor of Scarlatti's music. The damper pedal is not needed, because its effects were not possible during Scarlatti's time and therefore not intended.

ORNAMENTATION

The ornaments used in this book are the appoggiatura, trill, schleifer, turn and mordent. The realizations in light print above the staffs show how to play them. The basic rules for playing baroque ornaments are summarized below:

> Ornaments are written in small notes or in symbols above notes.

> Ornaments begin *on the beat* of the main (full size) note, and take their time value away from the main note.

- *Appoggiaturas* (♪) are accented and the main note played more softly.

- *Trills* 𝆑𝆑 begin on the next higher scale note, called the upper auxiliary.

  Trills must have at least 4 notes, but more may be added to them.

  Some trills have termination notes after them ♫. These little notes are played just as fast as the trill.

- *Schleifer* ♫ means "slide." The notes must sound as if they are sliding into place.

- The *turn* (∽) is played gracefully, ornamenting its main note with both upper and lower auxiliaries.

- The *mordent* (⸾) or "biting" ornament is incisive and uses a lower auxiliary.